BREAD
FOR HUNGRY CHRISTIANS

Frank Hamrick & Jerry Dean

PositiveAction
BIBLE CURRICULUM

Bread: For Hungry Christians

Written by Frank Hamrick and Jerry Dean

Copyright 1977, 2009 by Positive Action For Christ, Inc., P.O. Box 700, 502 W. Pippen Street, Whitakers, NC 27891. All rights reserved. No part may be reproduced in any manner without permission in writing from the publisher.

Second Edition

Printed in the United States of America

ISBN: 978-1-59557-114-4

Edited by C.J. Harris
Designed by Shannon Brown
Cover Artwork by Chris Ellison

Published by

TABLE OF CONTENTS

And Jesus said unto them, I am the bread of life: he that cometh to Me shall never hunger; and he that believeth on Me shall never thirst. (John 6:35)

Bread is one staple food every civilization needs. It is a basic food source required to sustain life.

It is significant that Jesus Christ presented Himself as the "bread come down from heaven." As the children of Israel hungered in the wilderness and were sent manna from the Father, so also is the soul of man satisfied by Jesus Christ, the true and living Bread. The world searches for that which can bring peace and contentment, and still there is restlessness within. They seek and find not; they thirst and find no refreshment for their parched, dry souls. Christ Jesus, the Bread of Life, alone can quench the thirst and fill the heart of unregenerate man. Only He can fill the void caused by sin.

This booklet is a study of our Savior. It is written for those who are hungry for the things of God. In Matthew 5 we read, "Blessed are they which do hunger and thirst after righteousness: for they shall be filled." As you read and study the life of Christ, it is our desire that you will see Him in a new light and that He will become dearer and more precious to you. Christ has done more than our mortal minds can ever comprehend; yet, the Word provides us with a beautiful picture of His life, death, and present work. To the Christian, He truly is Bread, the daily sustenance.

Before you begin your study, however, why not pause and ask God to give you a fresh look at His Son and His finished work. Ask Him to thrill your heart anew with the wonderful salvation and joyous, abundant life He has provided in Himself. Now may God bless you as you study His infallible Word.

1

CHRIST:
HIS PRE–EXISTENCE

In this chapter we will study the pre–incarnate Christ.

What does pre–incarnate mean?

The word *pre–incarnate* is really two words put together. *Pre* means before. *Incarnate* means in the flesh. Thus, the preincarnation of Christ speaks of the time before Christ came in the flesh to earth.

Since Christ is called the Son of God, wasn't He created by God?

Let's see what the Bible says about Christ's pre–existence (before He came to earth).

Creator and Sustainer

- We have already studied this verse in the *Meat* booklet, but look again at Genesis 1:26. What does the personal pronoun "us" indicate? _____
_____
_____

We have seen in our study of the Trinity and the Holy Spirit that God's Spirit aided in creation.

But that doesn't mean Christ did too!

- Turn to John 1:1–2. Who is the Word mentioned in these verses (see verse 14)?_____

- Now look at verse 3. What did He do? _____
_____

- Turn to Hebrews 1:2. According to this verse, by whom did God create the world? _____

- Now read Colossians 1:15–17. What does this passage state about Christ? _____
  _____
  _____

- Notice especially verse 17. What two things are said about Christ?

  1. _____
     _____

  2. _____
     _____

- What does this fact that all things are held together (consist) by Christ teach us about Him? _____
  _____

Thus, we see that Christ is the Creator and Sustainer of the universe.

> *But couldn't Christ have been created*
> *before the earth was created?*

From Everlasting to Everlasting

- Turn to John 1:1–2. What do these verses plainly state about Christ (in your own words)?_____
  _____
  _____

- Now look at Micah 5:2. Though Christ was born in Bethlehem, did He begin there? _____

- How long has He existed? _____
  _____

- See also John 17:5. How does Christ ask God to glorify Him? _____

_____

_____

_____

Jesus also claimed His own pre–existence.

- Look at Exodus 3:14. God is giving Moses instructions so that he will be accepted by the Israelites as their leader. Who did God tell Moses to say sent him? _____

The Hebrew word for "I am" is a name for God that was so revered and holy that the Jews would not even speak it!

- Now look at John 8:58. What did Jesus say here?

_____

- What did He mean by that?_____

_____

_____

_____

- How did the people respond when Jesus equated Himself with God (verse 59)? _____

_____

- Turn to Revelation 1:8. What did Christ say regarding Himself in this verse? _____

_____

_____

_____

_____

The Scriptures plainly teach that Jesus Christ, the Son of God, has existed with and in the Father in eternity past, in the present, and will continue to do so in the future. He is equal with God in every respect and merely lowered Himself, taking the form of a human being so that you and I might be redeemed! What a great God and Savior we have!

Complete This Section Without Looking Back at the Lesson

1. Define pre–incarnation. _____
   _____
   _____

2. What does John 1:1–3 teach concerning Christ?
   _____
   _____
   _____

3. What two things does Colossians 1:17 teach us about Christ? _____
   _____
   _____
   _____

4. According to John 17:5, what did Christ share with the Father in eternity past? _____
   _____

5. What did Jesus mean when He said, "I am"?
   _____
   _____
   _____
   _____

Verses to Memorize

- Colossians 1:16-17
- John 8:58

2

CHRIST:
HIS VIRGIN BIRTH

When we say that Christ was born of a virgin, we mean that He was born of a woman but had no human father.

First, let's look at prophetic Scripture.

Doom Pronounced upon Man

Turn to Genesis 3:14–15. Here we read the very first prophecy in the Bible.

- To whom is the Lord God speaking? _____

- Who is the serpent? _____

- Who is the woman in verse 15? _____

- What would be the attitude of the devil and the woman toward each other from this point on? _____
  _____

- But notice the latter part of verse 15. The verse says that there will not only be conflict between the serpent and the woman but also between whom? _____
  _____

- Who is the woman's offspring or seed mentioned in verse 15? _____
  _____

- So there would also be conflict between whom?
  _____

A Deliverer Promised

Now notice the pronoun "her" in verse 15. This is a key word. Everywhere else in the Bible a different pronoun is used when speaking of descendants. Look up these verses: Genesis 46:6, Psalm 18:50, Isaiah 53:10.

- What pronoun is used in each verse? _____

- We can see by these verses that there was to be a future descendant of Eve who would be different from all other humans. He would be of the seed (offspring) of woman and not of man. The rest of Genesis 3:15 tells us what this unique individual would do. Notice first, whose head would be bruised (crushed)?_____

- Now, notice again the personal pronoun in the last phrase. What will Satan do to the seed (offspring) of the woman? _____

   So, we see here that the seed of the woman is a person who will bruise the head of Satan.

What does it mean to bruise someone's head?

- Christ mortally "bruised" Satan when He died on Calvary and rose again the third day. Christ has brought victory over the devil! But the key point to keep in mind is that Christ is the "seed (offspring)_____," prophesying the virgin birth.

- Turn to another prophetic Scripture, Isaiah 7:14. In this passage it is plainly stated that a virgin shall conceive and bear a son. What will this child's name be? _____

- Now turn to Matthew 1:23–25. Who is this prophesied virgin–born child? _____

- Notice also what Luke, a very competent physician, says in Luke 1:30–38. What does the key verse (37) say?

  _____

  _____

> What difference does it make? Christ could be the Savior and not be virgin–born, couldn't He?

The Bible's Credibility Hinges on It

- If Christ were not born of a virgin, how would that affect the reliability of the Scriptures? _____

  _____

  _____

Christ's Sinlessness Is a Factor

- Secondly, you remember we studied the doctrine of man in the *Meat* booklet. Briefly, in your own words, what does Romans 5:12–14 mean? _____

  _____

  _____

  _____

- That's true. Every descendant of Adam has sinned. We've already seen that another word for descendant is what (Gen. 3:15)? _____

- Since Christ was not of the seed (offspring) of Adam, does Romans 5:12 apply to Him? _____

- Why or why not? _____

  _____

  _____

_____

_____

> *Since Christ wasn't born of the seed of man, He didn't inherit Adam's sinful nature. Therefore, Christ is the only human who ever lived who wasn't a sinner!*

- In your own words, what does 2 Corinthians 5:21 tell us about Christ? _____

  _____

  _____

  _____

- Also, state what 1 Peter 3:18 means to those who are God's children._____

  _____

  _____

  _____

> *If Christ had been naturally–born, He would have been a sinner and couldn't have died for anyone else's sins.*

That's right! Christ's virgin birth makes it possible for us to have a sinless, perfect Savior who could die for our sins in our place.

Complete This Section Without Looking Back at the Lesson

1. Define virgin birth. _____
    _____
    _____

2. What does Genesis 3:15 tell us about relationship between the seed (offspring) of the woman and the seed of the serpent? _____
    _____
    _____
    _____

3. How did Christ "bruise Satan's head"? _____
    _____
    _____
    _____

4. Why is it absolutely necessary that Christ be virgin–born?
    _____
    _____
    _____
    _____
    _____
    _____

Verses to Memorize

- Genesis 3:15
- Isaiah 7:14

3
CHRIST: HIS PURPOSE IN COMING

There are many modern views of the purpose for Christ's coming and death on the cross. Let's look first at the false views of Christ's coming and death.

Unscriptural Views of Christ's Coming and Death

The Accident Theory

> Christ's death was an accident. He never intended to die on a cross.

First of all, it was prophesied that Christ would die. Look up the following Old Testament passages and match each verse with the corresponding description of Christ's death made many years before He actually came to earth.

1. _____ Psalm 22:7   A. Despised by the people

2. _____ Psalm 22:6   B. Rejected by men

3. _____ Isaiah 53:7   C. Divided garments

4. _____ Isaiah 53:3   D. Laughed to scorn; mocked

5. _____ Psalm 22:18   E. Thirty pieces of silver

6. _____ Zechariah 11:12   F. Wounded for our transgressions

7. _____ Isaiah 53:5   G. Bones out of joint

8. _____ Psalm 22:14   H. Pierced hands and feet

9. _____ Isaiah 53:4   I. With rich in death

10. _____ Psalm 22:15   J. Lamb led to slaughter

11. _____ Isaiah 53:9   K. Smitten by God

12. _____ Psalm 22:16   L. Tongue cleaves to jaws

- What do these Scriptures prove about Christ's coming?
  _____
  _____

- Notice also, Christ told of His approaching death. Read Matthew 16:21, Mark 9:30–32, and John 10:17–18 and state in your own words what Christ said. _____
  _____
  _____
  _____

- If Christ knew so much about His death and resurrection beforehand, could it have been an accident? _____

The Martyr Theory

> *Christ was killed because He was faithful to His principles and to what He considered His duty. We are to learn faithfulness to truth and duty from Him. His example is to teach man to repent of his sins and to reform.*

This view of Christ's death teaches that salvation comes through following the example of Christ.

- Look up the following verses and state how we are saved.

  1. Ephesians 2:8a _____
     _____

  2. 1 Peter 1:18–19 _____
     _____

  3. John 1:12 _____
     _____

- In the following verses we are told to follow Christ's example (1 John 2:6; 1 Pet. 2:21, 24; Matt. 11:29). To whom were these verses written? _____

_____

- Is it possible for an unsaved person to follow Christ's perfect example? _____

- Why or why not? (Give Scripture to prove your answer.)

_____

_____

_____

_____

- If Christ's death was nothing more than that of a martyr, then His death is no more meaningful than Stephen's death or that of any other martyr. What does Peter say about Christ in Acts 4:12 that proves Christ's death to be more than a martyr's death? _____

_____

_____

The Governmental Theory

> *The benevolence of God requires that He make an example of suffering in Christ in order to show man that sin is displeasing in His sight. God's government of the world necessitates that He show His wrath against sin.*

- It is true that God is displeased with the sin of man. But what kind of person did God choose to show His displeasure against sin? See 2 Corinthians 5:21 and 1 Peter 3:18.

_____

Isn't it strange that God would choose an innocent person to show His displeasure for the sins of a guilty human race!

The Love of God Theory

> *Christ died to show men how much God loved them! From then on men would know the feeling of the heart of God toward them. He died to communicate man's real worth to God.*

It's true that God did demonstrate His love by sending Christ to die (Rom. 5:8; John 3:16), but men did not need such a sacrifice to know that God loved them. They knew this before Christ came! Psalm 103 is a praise to God for His love for the Israelites long before the time of Christ.

- Again, look at 2 Corinthians 5:21. Why does this verse say Christ was made sin for us'? _____
  _____
  _____

- What reason does 1 Peter 3:18 give for Christ's death?__
  _____
  _____

  _____

Christ's death reveals God's love, but God's love is not the reason for Christ's death.

Biblical Reasons for Christ's Coming and Death

Now let's see the biblical reasons for Christ's coming.

He Came to Fulfill the Promises of God

- After each reference list the prophecy that Christ fulfilled.

  1. Genesis 3:15

     _____

2. Isaiah 7:14

_____

3. Micah 5:2

_____

4. Isaiah 9:6

_____

5. Zechariah 11:13–14

_____

6. Isaiah 53:12

_____

He Came to Reveal the Father

- State in your own words what John 1:18 and 14:9 mean.

_____

_____

_____

He Came to Become a Faithful High Priest

Christ came in the flesh so that He could understand our condition, situation, and temptations and be qualified as a faithful High Priest.

- Read Hebrews 5:1–2 and write, in your own words, how and why the Old Testament high priests were chosen. _

_____

_____

_____

_____

- As you understand it, what does Hebrews 2:17–18 mean?

_____

_____

_____

- Also, what does Hebrews 4:15–16 mean? _____

  _____

  _____

  _____

He Came to Put Away Sin

- Read Hebrews 9:26. In your own words, what does the
  end of the verse say that Christ did? _____

  _____

  _____

- Turn to 1 John 3:5. What does this verse mean?

  _____

  _____

- What does Mark 10:45 say was Christ's purpose in coming to earth? _____

  _____

  _____

He Came to Destroy the Works of the Devil

- Read 1 John 3:8b and state why the Son of God was
  manifested. _____

  _____

  _____

- What does Hebrews 2:14–15 mean? _____

  _____

  _____

  _____

He Came to Give Us an Example of a Holy Life

- Though Christ did not state that He came for the specific purpose of giving us an example, that purpose is strongly implied in the Scriptures. What do the following verses instruct us to do?

    1.1 John 2:6 _____

    _____

    2.1 Peter 2:21 _____

    _____

He Came to Prepare for the Second Coming.

The salvation we have through the sacrifice of Christ saves us now from the power, penalty, and guilt of sin. Yet you and I are still forced to exist in this sinful world with all of its temptations and evil. Christ's salvation assures us that He will one day return and rapture the redeemed unto Himself, freeing us finally from the very presence of sin!

- How does Paul describe his earthly condition and heavenly hope in Romans 8:22–23? _____

    _____

    _____

    _____

    _____

Complete This Section Without Looking Back at the Lesson

- List the four false views of Christ's coming and death; then refute each with Scripture.

  1. _____
     _____
     _____

  2. _____
     _____
     _____

  3. _____
     _____
     _____

  4. _____
     _____
     _____

- List the seven reasons Christ came to earth to die; then give Scripture to prove your answer.

  1. _____
     _____
     _____

  2. _____
     _____
     _____

  3. _____
     _____
     _____

4. _____

_____

_____

5. _____

_____

_____

6. _____

_____

_____

7. _____

_____

_____

Verses to Memorize

- Hebrews 4:15
- 2 Corinthians 5:21

4

CHRIST:
HIS CHARACTER

The Bible is quite clear as to Christ's character, the kind of person He really was in everyday life. Let's look at the character of the Savior.

Christ Was Holy

- He was called holy. Look up the following verses and write beside each the biblical title given to Christ.

    1. Luke 1:35_____

    2. Mark 1:24 _____

    3. Luke 2:23_____

    4. Acts 3:14 _____

    5. Acts 2:27 _____

    6. Acts 4.27 _____

    7. Acts 4:30 _____

What does the word holy mean anyway?

- In your own words, write a definition of the word *holy*.

    _____

    _____

    _____

- How does the dictionary define holy? _____

    _____

    _____

    _____

In reference to Christ, the word *holy* means perfect, sinless, without fault. He had a holy nature. Look at John 14:30 and answer the following questions.

- Who is speaking? _____

- Who is the prince and ruler of this world? _____

- In your own words, what does the last phrase mean?

  _____

  _____

- The last phrase actually means that Satan had absolutely no power over any phase of Christ's nature and life. We have already seen how the devil controls all other men, but in Christ he has nothing! What phrase in Hebrews 4:15 further proves Christ's holy nature? _____

  _____

He was holy in conduct. Hebrews 7:26 states that Christ was separate from sinners.

- What does this mean? _____

  _____

Christ never followed the ways of man. He never sinned! He always did those things that pleased His Father.

- Read John 8:29b. What does it mean? _____

  _____

  _____

Christ Had Genuine Love

- Look up the following passages and tell whom Christ loved and how that love was revealed.

1. John 15:13; Romans 5:8 _____

    _____

    _____

2. Ephesians 5:2, 25 _____

    _____

    _____

3. John 15:9 _____

    _____

4. Luke 23:32–36; Matthew 5:43–48 _____

    _____

    _____

Christ Was Humble

- Look up the verses and state in your own words how Christ humbled Himself.

    1. Philippians 2:5–8 _____

        _____

        _____

        _____

    2. 2 Corinthians 8:9 _____

        _____

        _____

    3. Luke 2:7 _____

        _____

    4. Luke 9:58 _____

        _____

    5. Matthew 20:28 _____

        _____

6. John 13:14 _____

_____

He Had a Meaningful, Consistent Prayer Life

- When did Christ pray?

  1. Luke 6:12 _____

  2. Mark 1:35 _____

  3. Matthew 26:38–46 _____

  4. John 6:15–16 _____

If Christ, the holy Son of God, needed to pray so much, what about us?

He Worked Steadily at What God Had for Him to Do

- State, in your own words, what Christ meant in John 9:4.

  _____

  _____

  _____

- When did Christ's day begin (Mark 1:35; John 8:2)? ____

  _____

- When did it end (Matthew 8:16; John 3:2)? _____

  _____

- When Christ was doing God's work, what things did He forget?

  1. John 4:31–34 _____

  2. Mark 6:31–34 _____

  3. Luke 23:40–43 _____

- Read 1 Peter 2:21 and 1 John 2:6. What are we instructed to do? _____

  _____

  _____

- What was Paul's desire for the Christians of Galatia in Galatians 4:19? _____

  _____

  _____

- What does that mean? _____

  _____

But, how can I be like Christ?

In John 15, Christ presents Himself as the true vine and Christians as the branches. We must remember that Christ, our Life, gives us the power and strength to follow His steps. Yet we must "abide" or "remain" in Him. We must daily focus our minds and thoughts on Him. As we seek Him, God provides the guidance and strength to overcome our sinful flesh and follow Him.

- Read Galatians 5:22–23. As we yield to the Holy Spirit, what characteristics of Christ will be produced in our lives? _

  _____

  _____

  _____

Have you surrendered your life anew to the Lord today? Are you as close to the Lord as you once were? Why not kneel, right now, confessing your sins to the Lord and yield your body afresh to His control!

Complete This Section Without Looking Back at the Lesson

- What are the five elements of Christ's character studied in this chapter?

  1. _____
     _____

  2. _____
     _____

  3. _____
     _____

  4. _____
     _____

  5. _____
     _____

- What does the word *holy* mean? _____
  _____
  _____

- In what ways was Christ holy? _____
  _____
  _____
  _____

- What verse proves that Christ demonstrated His love for sinners by dying for them? _____

- Where do we get the strength to live a life of Christlikeness?
  _____

Verses to Memorize

- 1 Peter 2:21
- John 15:4

5
CHRIST:
HIS SINLESS LIFE

> *I know that the Bible calls Christ "holy," but that doesn't really say He was sinless. Why is Christ's sinlessness so important?*

- We have studied the deity of Christ in the *Meat* booklet, and in the *Bread* booklet we have studied Christ's character, virgin birth, and purpose for coming. State in your own words the answer to the question above and give scriptural proof for your answers. _____

_____

_____

_____

_____

_____

More than Holy

- The Bible does say more than just that Christ was holy. Look up the following verses and list the word or words that reveal Christ's character.

  1. 1 Peter 1:19 _____

  2. Zechariah 9:9 _____

  3. Isaiah 53:11 _____

  4. Acts 22:14 _____

  5. John 8:46 _____

  6. Matthew 27:3-4 _____

  7. Hebrews 7:26 _____

  8. 1 Peter 2:22 _____

  9. John 5:30 _____

  10. 2 Corinthians 5:21 _____

  11. James 1:13–14 _____

12. Isaiah 53:9 _____

13. John 7:18 _____

14. Hebrews 1:9 _____

15. 1 John 5:20 _____

> *Yes, but Christ is God. Sin and temptations didn't affect Him like they do me.*

- Turn to Hebrews 4:15. Who is the High Priest?
  _____

- In your own words, what does the latter part of the verse mean? _____
  _____
  _____
  _____

> *But why did Christ allow Himself to be tested and tempted so greatly?*

- Look at Hebrews 2:16–18. According to verse 16a, in what form could Christ have come to earth?
  _____

- What form did Christ choose to take when He came to earth?
  _____
  _____

- According to verse 17, why was it important for Christ to be made like unto other men? _____
  _____
  _____
  _____

Look closely at verse 18. Here it says Christ was tempted so that He might be a help to those who are tempted.

- Now explain verses 16-18 in your own words.

_____

_____

_____

_____

_____

_____

> *So Christ came and lived in the flesh, suffering the same temptations I do, that He might better understand my problems? It's hard to believe He'd do that for me!*

Yes, it's hard to believe, but Christ did live in this sin-cursed world, being tempted on every hand so that He might understand our feelings and be a faithful High Priest.

Have you recently thanked God for His faithful Son who not only died, but lived on earth for you, "yet without sin"? Why not stop a moment and thank Him?

Complete This Section Without Looking Back at the Lesson

- Why is it necessary to our faith that Christ be sinless?

_____

_____

_____

- List six references that show Christ's sinlessness.

1. _____

_____

2. _____

_____

3. _____

_____

4. _____

_____

5. _____

_____

6. _____

_____

- Why did Christ allow Himself to be tempted and tested by sin? _____

_____

_____

- What verse states Christ was tempted in all the ways we are?

_____

_____

- What does it mean that Christ is able to help those who are tempted? _____

_____

_____

_____

Verse to Memorize

- Hebrews 2:18

6
CHRIST:
HIS DEATH

- Let's go back to Genesis 2:17. What was God's command?

  _____

  _____

  _____

- What was the penalty for disobedience? _____

  _____

- We have already studied that we have all followed Adam's rebellious example. What verses state that every man is a sinner by nature? _____

- What, since Eden, has God demanded as a payment for sin?_____

- Could God righteously forgive any sin without requiring the death of the sinner? _____

So, again, we see the terrible plight of sinful man: lost, condemned to die with no hope of escape.

But, there is hope—in Christ!

The Vicarious Atonement

Now we can begin to see the importance of Christ's death. As guilty sinners, we needed a righteous substitute to take our place. In Christ we have the vicarious atonement.

Vicarious atonement, what does that mean?

- Look up the word *vicar* in the dictionary and give a one–word definition. _____

Thus, we have a substitute atonement.

But what does atonement mean?

- Turn to Romans 5 and read verses 8–11. When did God demonstrate (show) His love toward us? _____

  _____

- Look closely at verses 9 and 10. Verse 9 says sinners are justified how? _____

  _____

- How does verse 10 say God's enemies were reconciled to Himself?_____

  _____

The two words mentioned above may be defined thusly:

1. Justified—made innocent of all sin
2. Reconciled—restored to favor with God

- Look at verse 11. Through Christ, what have we received?

  _____

- So, by what act is atonement or reconciliation provided?

  _____

  _____

Vicarious atonement is the act whereby Christ substituted for the sinner and paid the price for that sinner, bringing forgiveness from and peace with a holy God. So, we can see that salvation is not brought about by the example of Christ, or by anything we can do. Since God's justice demanded death, Christ rightly satisfied those demands.

Christ's Death Is the Basis of the Gospel

- Notice 1 Corinthians 15:1a. What is Paul declaring to the Corinthians?_____
  _____

- Since Paul is declaring the gospel—the good news of salvation—what is the very first thing he mentions in verse 3?
  _____

Paul realized that Christ's death for sinners was the basis of the gospel message.

- Turn to Revelation 5:8–10. Who is the Lamb? _____

- In your own words, What is the "new song" the saved will sing throughout eternity, according to verses 9 and 10? _
  _____
  _____
  _____
  _____
  _____
  _____

What a picture this is! Our song forever will be "worthy is the Lamb that was slain." The death of Christ is of utmost importance on earth and in heaven.

> **But was it His death that was so important, or was it the way in which He died that was important?**

- Read Hebrews 9:22. What is required for the remission (forgiveness) of sins?_____

- According to this verse, is Christ's death the important thing, or is it the way which He died that is important?
  _____

- Why? _____
  _____
  _____

Why Christ Died on a Cross

There are two basic reasons why Christ had to die on a cross and could not die some other way. Let's discover those two reasons.

1. Read Genesis 4:1–4. In light of Hebrews 9:22, why did God accept Abel's offering and reject Cain's offering? __
    _____
    _____

    - Read Exodus 12:1–13. What was the token that God had to see on each house to save that household from the death of the oldest son? _____

    - Thus, Christ had to die in a way that would shed His blood. A natural death or a death that would not shed blood could not atone for our sins. Read Romans 5:8-9. These verses tell us that Christ died for us, but what was it about His death that justifies us? _____
      _____

2. A second reason Christ had to die on the cross is because this was the method God had chosen and the method He had prophesied thousands of years before it happened.

    - Read Psalm 22:1–18. Record below the prophecies in this passage that described Christ's death on the cross:

    1. Verse 1 _____
        _____

2. Verse 7 _____

_____

3. Verse 14 _____

_____

4. Verse 15 _____

_____

5. Verse 16 _____

_____

6. Verse 18 _____

_____

This is just one of many Old Testament prophecies concerning the death of Christ. Thus, Christ had to die on the cross, not only to shed His blood, but also in fulfillment of the Scriptures.

- Read Mark 14:43–50. Christ stated that the soldiers had had many opportunities to capture and to kill Him, but they had not done so until now. What, according to this passage, was the reason they had not captured Christ and killed Him some other way?_____

_____

- Thus, there are two major reasons Christ died on the cross and not some other way. What are they?

  1. _____

  _____

  2. _____

  _____

Complete This Section Without Looking Back at the Lesson

- What is God's penalty for sin? What verses prove this fact?

  _____

  _____

- Why did Christ have to die? _____

  _____

  _____

- What does the word *justified* mean? _____

  _____

  _____

- What does the word *reconciled* mean?_____

  _____

  _____

- Define vicarious atonement. _____

  _____

  _____

  _____

- What reference shows that Paul considered the death of Christ the very basis of the gospel message? _____

- What will be the saints' eternal song?_____

  _____

- What are the two basic reasons Christ had to die on a cross?

  1. _____

     _____

  2. _____

     _____

Verses to Memorize

- Romans 5:8–10

7
CHRIST:
HIS RESURRECTION

> *I've heard that His disciples stole the body and then lied about the resurrection! Is there really proof that Christ rose bodily from the dead?*

The Importance of the Resurrection

Many people overlook the importance of the resurrection of Christ to the Christian faith. Christianity is the only religion that claims the bodily resurrection of its founder.

- Turn to 1 Corinthians 15. Notice verses 14, 17, and 18. What three things would result if Christ had not risen from the dead?

    1. _____
       _____

    2. _____
       _____

    3. _____
       _____

> *Some say Christ never really died but was drugged to appear dead!*

Christ Actually Died

- Look up the following verses and record the fact proving Christ's death.

    1. John 19:32–34 (a physiological proof that He was dead)
       _____
       _____

    2. Matthew 27:57–60 _____
       _____
       _____

3. Mark 15:44–45 _____

_____

_____

4. Mark 16:1 _____

_____

_____

5. Revelation 1:8 _____

_____

_____

What facts prove that Christ actually rose from the dead?

The Empty Tomb

- Look up these verses and state the proofs for the bodily resurrection. Matthew 28:6; Mark 16:6; Luke 24:3, 12; John 20:1-2 _____

_____

_____

_____

If Christ had not risen, the Romans would gladly have produced His body as evidence. But they could not—the tomb was empty.

But the disciples could have stolen the body of Jesus!

- Look at Matthew 27:62–66. What precautions did the Roman government take to keep the disciples from stealing Christ's body?_____

_____

_____

- Now notice what took place after Christ's resurrection. Read Matthew 28:11–15 and state what happened in your own words. _____

_____

_____

If the disciples had stolen His body, they would have known they were preaching a hoax. Why, then, would they have suffered such awful martyrdom (tradition tells us they were killed in various ways: boiled in oil, decapitated, crucified, stoned, and beaten) for something they knew was a hoax?!

Eyewitness Accounts

- Read these verses and record who saw the Lord.

    1. Mark 16:9–11 _____

    2. Matthew 28:1–10 _____

    3. Luke 24:34_____

    4. Luke 24:36–43_____

    5. John 20:26–31 _____

    6. John 21:1–6, 14_____

    7. Matthew 28:16–20 _____

    8. 1 Corinthians 15:7_____

    9. 1 Corinthians 15:6_____

Each appearance is recorded as an eyewitness account!

Perhaps they only saw a ghost.

- From the following verses describe the body of Jesus as seen by the witnesses.

1. John 20:19 _____

_____

2. John 20:14 _____

_____

3. Luke 24:36–43 _____

_____

4. John 20:20 _____

_____

5. John 20:24–29 _____

_____

What are the results of Christ's resurrection?

- Look up the following passages and list the results of Christ's resurrection.

  1. Romans 1:4; Acts 17:31 _____

  _____

  2. Romans 4:25 _____

  _____

  3. Romans 8:34 _____

  _____

  4. Ephesians 1:19–22 _____

  _____

  5. 1 Thessalonians 4:14 _____

  _____

  6. Acts 17:31 _____

  _____

Complete This Section Without Looking Back at the Lesson

- What would be the result if Christ had not risen from the dead? _____

  _____

  _____

  _____

  _____

  _____

- What proofs can you give that Christ actually died?

  _____

  _____

  _____

  _____

  _____

- What proves that Christ actually rose from the dead?

  _____

  _____

  _____

  _____

- List at least five different accounts of Christ being seen alive after His resurrection and give references for each one.

  1. _____

     _____

  2. _____

     _____

  3. _____

     _____

4. _____
   _____

5. _____
   _____

- What proves Christ was not a ghost? _____
  _____
  _____
  _____
  _____

- What are the six results of Christ's resurrection?

  1. _____
     _____

  2. _____
     _____

  3. _____
     _____

  4. _____
     _____

  5. _____
     _____

  6. _____
     _____

Verses to Memorize

- 1 Corinthians 15:13-14
- 1 Corinthians 15:20
- 1 Corinthians 15:55–57

8
CHRIST:
HIS ASCENSION
AND EXALTATION

The ascension was that event in the life of Christ when He departed visibly from His disciples into heaven. The exaltation is that act whereby the risen and ascended Christ is given a place of power and honor at the Father's right hand.

Christ's Ascension

What do the Scriptures say about the ascension?

- Look up the following passages and place them beside the correct event: Acts 7:55–56; Mark 16:19; Luke 24:50–51; John 6:61–62; 16:10; 20:17; 1 Timothy 3:16; 1 Peter 3:22.

    1. Christ foretells His ascension. _____

    2. New Testament writers record it. _____
    _____

    3. Stephen saw the exalted Christ. _____

    4. Peter preached it. _____

    5. Paul preached it. _____

- Read Acts 1:9–11 and, in your own words, state what happened. _____
_____
_____
_____
_____

But where did He go?

- Read Ephesians 4:10, Hebrews 4:14, and 7:26. According to these verses, where did Christ go? _____

- Look up the following verses and state what Christ is doing presently and the purpose of His ascension and exaltation.

    1. Hebrews 9:24 with 1 John 2:1 _____
    _____
    _____

    2. John 14:2 _____
    _____

    3. Hebrews 4:14–16 _____
    _____

    4. Ephesians 4:10 _____
    _____

Christ's Exaltation

What do the Scriptures say about the exaltation?

- Look up the following passages and summarize, in your own words, how Christ is exalted. Some will be present and some will be future events.

    1. Philippians 2:9-11 _____
    _____
    _____

    2. 1 Corinthians 15:24-27 _____
    _____
    _____

3. Hebrews 7:24-26 _____

_____

_____

4. Revelation 5:11-14 _____

_____

_____

- Look again at 1 Corinthians 15:24-27. Now read the next verse. What will Christ ultimately do when all things are brought under His authority? _____

_____

Even in Christ's exaltation, the glory will ultimately go to the Father. Thus the ultimate goal of the exaltation is that "God may be all in all."

> ### What do Christ's ascension and exaltation mean to the Christian?

- Again, look up these verses and state the results of Christ's ascension and exaltation.

    1. Hebrews 4:14–16 _____

    _____

    2. Colossians 1:18-19 _____

    _____

    3. Ephesians 1:20–22 _____

    _____

Complete This Section Without Looking Back at the Lesson

- Define ascension and exaltation.

    - Ascension _____

    _____

- Exaltation_____
  _____

- List five different people who spoke of Christ's ascension
  and exaltation and give a Scripture reference for each.

  1. _____
     _____

  2. _____
     _____

  3. _____
     _____

  4. _____
     _____

  5. _____
     _____

- Where is Christ now, and what is He doing? _____
  _____
  _____

- What benefits (results) of Christ's ascension and exaltation
  does the Christian receive? _____
  _____
  _____

Verses to Memorize

- Acts 1:10–11
- Hebrews 9:24

EXAMINATION QUESTIONS

Answer the following questions without looking back in your book for answers.

1. In Colossians 1:17, what does it mean that all things are held together (consist) by Christ? _____

   _____

   _____

2. Define the pre–Incarnation of Christ. _____

   _____

   _____

3. Write from memory John 8:58. _____

   _____

   _____

4. How did Christ bruise Satan's head? _____

   _____

   _____

5. Define the virgin birth. _____

   _____

6. Why is it absolutely necessary that Christ be virgin–born?

   _____

   _____

   _____

   _____

7. List seven reasons Christ came to earth to die and give Scripture references to prove your answer.

- _____

- _____

- _____

- _____

- _____

- _____

- _____

8. Write from memory Isaiah 7:14. _____
_____
_____
_____

9. What verse proves that Christ demonstrated His love for sinners by dying for them? _____

10. Write from memory Hebrews 4:15. _____
_____
_____
_____

11. What verse tells us that the seed (offspring) of the woman, Eve, will defeat the serpent, Satan? _____

12. Write from memory 2 Corinthians 5:21. _____
_____
_____
_____

13. Why is it necessary to our faith that Christ be sinless? _____

_____

14. What verse states that Christ was tempted in all the ways we are? _____

15. Define justified. _____

_____

_____

16. Define reconciled. _____

_____

_____

17. Define vicarious atonement. _____

_____

_____

18. List two reasons Christ's death was by crucifixion.

• _____

• _____

19. List at least five different accounts of Christ being seen alive after His resurrection and give references for each one.

• _____

• _____

• _____

• _____

• _____

20. What are the six results of Christ's resurrection?

- _____
- _____
- _____
- _____
- _____
- _____

21. Write from memory 1 Corinthians 15:13–14. _____

_____
_____
_____

22. Define ascension and exaltation. _____

_____
_____
_____

23. Where is Christ now, and what is He doing? _____

_____
_____

24. Write from memory Hebrews 9:24. _____

_____
_____
_____

25. Why did Christ allow Himself to be tested and tempted by sin? _____

_____
_____
_____